A guide to walking

THE TWO COUNTIES WAY

from Taunton to Starcross

A Guide to Walking the Two Counties Way:
From Taunton to Starcross

Copyright © Trail Wanderer Publications 2018

www.trailwanderer.co.uk
contact@trailwanderer.co.uk

First Printed 2018

Printed ISBN 978-1-9999509-1-0
Digital ISBN 978-1-9999509-5-8

Cover Photo – Stefanie Gross @stefgphoto
All other photographs - Matthew Arnold
Editor - Scarlett Mansfield

Dedication

To Nan, Mum, Dad & Katie

Tiverton Bridge Car Park

TABLE OF CONTENTS

How To Use This Guide   1

General Introduction   4

    - What Is The Two Counties Way?

Characteristics of the Area   6

    - Taunton Deane

    - Exe Valley

    - Exeter And Exe Estuary

Wildlife & Vegetation   8

    - Canal Wildlife

    - Exe Estuary Wildlife

Weather   11

Preparation   11

    - Accommodation

    - Food & Nutrition

    - Village Pubs, Shops And Cafes

Navigation   15

    - Maps Covering The Route

    - Signposts & Waymarkers

Kit List   17

    - On Person

    - Personal Kit Carried in Pack

    - Additional Kit

Getting to the start point (Taunton)   20

    - By Rail

    - By Car

    - Buses

Leaving the Finishing Point (Starcross)   **21**

- By Rail

- By Car

- Buses

Distance Chart   **23**

- Height Elevation

The Route   **25**

Leg 1 - Taunton to Bradford-on-Tone   26

Leg 2 - Bradford-on-Tone to Wellington   34

Leg 3 - Wellington to Greenham   40

Leg 4 - Greenham to Sampford Peverell   46

Leg 5 - Sampford Peverell to Tiverton   52

Leg 6 - Tiverton to Bickleigh   58

Leg 7 - Bickleigh to Silverton   64

Leg 8 - Silverton to Broadclyst   70

Leg 9 - Broadclyst To Exeter (Quay)   76

Leg 10 - Exeter (Quay) to Starcross   88

Finishing At Starcross   100

Useful Information   **104**

- Organisations

- Public Transportation

- Community Information

- Taxis

- Additional Info

- Emergency Services

Notes: **108**

HOW TO USE THIS GUIDE

Owing to the fact that the Two Counties Way is not a recognised trail, it is consequently not displayed on OS mapping. This guide, therefore, has been written to provide you with full instructions on walking the entire length of this wonderful long-distance walking path. The following guide is broken down into a number of helpful sections in order to provide a more enjoyable experience.

Firstly, an introductory section will provide background information that contains a greater insight on the history and the profile of the terrain you will be traversing over, along with the abundance of wildlife that you may encounter.

Secondly, a preparation section, provides all the information on how to get to the start point, leaving the finishing point, travel information, distances between each of the major settlements and such like so that you can properly plan ahead to make your walk much more enjoyable.

Thirdly, and very importantly, is a detailed description of the whole route broken down into easily manageable legs. At the start of each section, you will find information on accommodation, pubs, and eateries. More importantly, this is where you will find detailed mapping.

Finally, at the back of the book, you will find a section titled 'Useful information' that provides the websites and contact details of the numerous organisations, groups, and travel information bureaus that you might find useful.

Sellake bridge, Grand Western Canal

GENERAL INTRODUCTION

WHAT IS THE TWO COUNTIES WAY?

The Two Counties Way trail winds for 90 kilometers / 56 miles from its start point in Taunton, Somerset, to its end at Starcross in Devon. It is important to note that it is not a recognized national trail rather it constitutes a number of footpaths, bridleways, and other long-distance routes including the West Deane Way, the Exe Valley Way, and the Southwest Coastal Path. It has a 1,220m (4,003 ft) ascent and a maximum height of 191m (627 ft).

The Two Counties Way enables you to venture through the best of British heritage and explore the remnants of our wonderful industrial past. Along the way, for example, walkers can enjoy taking the Grand Western Canal to Tiverton. This canal dates back to 1796. Initially, designers intended for the canal to link the Bristol Channel and the English Channel in order to bypass the delays and hazards of sailing around Land's End. Unfortunately, construction was never completed as the invention of railways removed the need for it.

The Tiverton to Lowdwells section of the canal became one of the first sections to be built despite being located in the middle; this was owing to the potential trade in limestone between quarries located in Canonsleigh and Tiverton and consequently the potential income this would generate. Way over budget at £224,505, this section of the canal finally opened in 1814. By 1904, only two boats were working on the canal. After 1925, the only income to be made on the canal came from charging farmers to wash their sheep and the sale of water lilies that grew in the area. In 1962, the British Transport Commission abandoned the canal and it remained unused until 1970 when the Devonshire County Council took control and opened a towpath as a country walk. Despite threats to its future, it is the only section to remain open and it has been designated a Country Park and a Local Nature Reserve.

Today, you can spend hours wandering around the canal and enjoying what the area has to offer. Alternatively, you can take a trip on a horse-drawn barge and enjoy the view from the water itself. You can also hire your own boats, take a picnic basket, and sit and simply watch the unique nature and wildlife in the surrounding area.

Another interesting encounter on this walk is the Tonedale Mills near to Wellington. Established during the middle of the eighteenth century as part of the booming industrial revolution, at its peak it was the largest woollen mill in South West England, producing around 6,500 meters of material each day and hiring 3,600 workers. It also famously developed the khaki dye used by the British Army. Today, the site is notable for possessing the remains of each phase of power generation: electricity, water, and steam. Owing to heavy low-cost competition from abroad, in the 1980s the factory severely downsized and most of the site has now been abandoned. It is definitely worth taking a trip to see these buildings shortly though as attempts to turn the site into housing are continuously being pushed through.

From Tiverton, the path proceeds through the Exe Valley and on to the towpath of Exeter's Ship canal down towards the Exe Estuary where you eventually join the more famous South West Coast Path whilst briefly venturing through the grounds of Powderham Castle to finaly arrive at Starcross.

CHARACTERISTICS OF THE AREA

TAUNTON DEANE

Starting in Taunton, this area of the route is mainly flat as it follows alongside the River Tone before taking you onto the canal towpath to Tiverton, via Bradford on Tone and Wellington.

To the north of Taunton lies the Quantock Hills in Somerset. Designated in 1956 as the first of England's 'Areas of Outstanding and Natural Beauty', the region provides gorgeous panoramic views over large areas of heathland, parklands, agricultural land, and oak woodlands. It is also the home of the Coleridge Way as the poet Samuel Coleridge, famous for co-founding the Romantic Movement, lived in the village of Nether Stowey from 1797 to 1799.

The Blackdown Hills are also to the South of Taunton along the Devon-Somerset border, and again, since 1991, this area has been designated an Area of Outstanding and Natural Beauty. Characterised by high plateaux's, deep valleys, and steep ridges, the hills are home to rare wildlife and stunning scenery. Human occupation dates back to the Iron Age and you can find the remains of motte-and-bailey castles, ancient hill forts, and even World War Two airfields.

Another landmark in this area is just outside of Wellington, on the edge of the Blackdown hills towards the other side of the M5. Along the trail when passing between Bradford-on-Tone and Wellington you can spot the towering 175-foot high triangular obelisk built to commemorate the Duke of Wellington's victory at the Battle of Waterloo. Completed in 1854, today it is owned by the National Trust and remains the tallest three-sided obelisk in the world.

Unfortunately, the site was closed to the public in 2007 after safety concerns were raised owing to the risk of falling stone debris which means you currently cannot access the internal staircase to rise to the viewing platform. However, extensive repair work is underway and it is hoped the monument will be reopened soon. A permanent solution to the deterioration of the monument though is expected to cost around £3.8 million and the National Trust are working on fundraising for this cause.

EXE VALLEY

On this part of the trail, walkers will follow along the beautiful scenic route and soaring hills carved out by the River Exe through the most glorious parts of Devon's countryside. The majority of this section follows quiet country lanes and footpaths but there are a few brief busy sections, such as through the 6,400 acre estate of Killerton, which is extremely popular with walkers and guest visiting the beautiful surroundings.

EXETER AND EXE ESTUARY

Venture on and head through Exeter's Historic Quayside, part of the city of Exeter. This area is also located next to the River Exe and the Exeter Ship Canal. The Quay was first used as a port in prehistoric times as an unloading point for overseas traders. In 1381, the river was blocked to ships but a canal was completed in 1566 to provide access once again. After the advent of the railway, it is now primarily used for leisure only – several fun events occur here every year. If you are lucky you can plan your trip to coincide with these events which include Dragon Boat Racing, Canoe races, night food markets, and craft fairs (to name a few). For TV buffs out there, Exeter Quay is also famous for being the filming location of the popular 1970s TV series 'Onedin Line' owing to the lack of modernisation around the area as it provided the perfect backdrop for a Victorian period drama.

While walking from Exeter to Starcross the final section will start to leave the more urban areas as you leave Exeter's Quayside and Canal Basin but most of it is still beautiful regardless. The central section meanwhile takes you through marshes and past a pound lock canal, built in the 1560s and England's oldest one. From here on you can start to enjoy the wildlife as this section of the Exe Estuary is an internationally recognised site designated to spot birdlife. Take your time and enjoy your success when you reach the end!

WILDLIFE & VEGETATION

CANAL WILDLIFE

The Grand Western Canal supports a wide variety of wildlife and vegetation with fantastic opportunities to get up close to nature. Hedgerows have been purposefully planted alongside the towpath in order to encourage and promote habitats for different plants, insects, mammals, and birds.

When it comes to plants, the canal comes alive in spring and summer owing to the copious number of wildflowers. Orchids grace the embankment while Yellow Flag Iris emerge alongside the water's edge as well. Thanks to this, there are also several different insects to enjoy, from the Water Boatmen and Damselfly to a variety of Butterflies and Dragonflies.

In the water, the canal is home to a number of different fish: from Carp and Pike to Tench, Perch, Bream and Roach, the canal offers a fun challenge to any prospective fishermen. Remember though, it is essential to gain an angling license from the Tiverton and District Angling Club with the current charge being £25 for an adult for a year, £12 for OAP/ Disabled, and £8 for children.

While most of the mammals can be hard to spot if you are lucky you will have the opportunity to see some unique characters in and around the water. The most elusive of all is the otter; if you see one on your route the Ranger service would love to know so that the sighting can be recorded (e-mail gwcanal@devon.gov. uk). Unfortunately, the water vole that once thrived on the canal has dramatically declined in recent years but efforts are underway to assist in their survival. More frequently, it is possible to see a wide variety of bats and you can actually go on a specific bat walk if you are in the area at the right time of the year. Finally, you can also spot Roe Deer, Badgers, and Foxes.

For those keen bird lovers among you, it is possible to see a wide variety along the route. Though Waterfowl, Mallards, Moorhens, and Mute Swans are the most common, if you look closely you can also see Kingfishers. Rarer sightings include Snipe, Little Grebe, Woodpeckers, and Water Railbirds. Of course, you can also see more common species such as Chaffinches, Robins, Blackbirds, Blue Tits, Greenfinches, and Song Thrushes.

EXE ESTUARY WILDLIFE

Typically estuaries provide a less than hospitable environment for animals to live in as changing tides require a certain level of adaptability. In order to see the most wildlife possible, it is best to google the tide times beforehand and consider what season you visit in. The mudflats, however, do offer some wildlife.

When it comes to mammals, if you look at the sandbanks throughout the Estuary you may be able to see a Grey Seal. Further, while in the upper estuary though they were once nearing extinction, it is common to find otters swimming along. If you are lucky, and visiting during some of the warmer months, around the Dawlish Warren area you may be able to spot a Sand Lizard – you are most likely to find them where there is a good mix of Marram grass and bare sand and before the day gets too hot.

Bird-wise, if you are visiting July through to March, you may be able to see a Dunlin feeding on the estuary mudflats or an Avocet towards the upper estuary. If you are around from September to March, you may see a Dark Bellied Brent Geese resting at high tide and feeding on the eelgrass that grows on intertidal areas of the Southern Estuary. Other birds in the area include Wigeons, Redshanks, Little Egrets, Ospreys, and Black-tailed.

Pitt Woods.

WEATHER

The best time of the year to walk the Two Counties Way largely depends on what you hope to see and find. Wildlife flourishes at all different times of the year and no specific month is particularly better than another unless there is something specific you want to see.

When it comes to temperature, February is the coldest month to visit while July is the hottest. Around Exeter, on average November to April get a high of 10 degrees and a low of 4 degrees Celsius. The weather starts to get warmer in May with an average high of 16 degrees and a low of 7 degrees but it really picks up from June to September with average highs of 20 degrees and lows on average of 11 degrees. October is somewhere between with a high of 15 degrees and a low of 8 degrees.

When it comes to rainfall, the wettest months to visit are from December to March with an average of 30mm of rain every month. April, September, October, and November all average 20mm while May to August averages only 10mm. Overall, January sees the highest average of rain days with 21 days a month, while June sees the least with an average of only 13 days of rain a month.

PREPARATION

ACCOMMODATION

As you pass along the Two Counties Way you will encounter a multitude of charming hotels, bed and breakfasts, and even campsites, to suit all tastes and budgets.

It is impossible to give credit to all of these sites but at the beginning of each leg, you will find a select number of accommodation sites listed as well as further contact information under the 'Useful Information' section on page 104. These have been chosen as they are specifically located near to the main trail but you should also remember to account for any added distance it may take should you wish to stop somewhere en route.

Of course, it is advisable to spend some time carrying out your own online research to find suitable stopover locations. Websites such as Booking.com and Airbnb also provide a great resource when looking for accommodation. They allow you to book a room in someone's home or guesthouse at a fraction of the cost of paying for a hotel; great if you plan on staying for only 1 night.

FOOD & NUTRITION

All of the villages that you will encounter along the Two Counties Way are situated in fairly close proximity so refuelling and stocking up on supplies is not going to present much of a problem. However, it is still important to plan for the entire length of your trip so that you have enough calories to sustain yourself; 56 miles is a hefty distance.

Ideally, you should consider each leg of your walk and think about what food you need that day to help you complete the distance required. This is one of the fun parts of preparing for the walk as it gives you a chance to be creative, consider what food goes well together, and perhaps even trying things you have not eaten before. You should also consider taking vitamins to supplement any lack of nutrients. It is a good idea to separate your food into days so you know exactly what you are having on each and do not run out of food faster than expected. If you have allowed yourself extra days for a detour, be sure to account for the energy needed to complete these sections too.

It is also vital to carry enough water to last you for each section. Generally, the elevation is fairly flat for the most part, that is until you reach the hills around Bickleigh and close to the Exe Valley; regardless, it is still important to take on enough fluids in order to allow your body to maintain an optimum working temperature.

If you plan on carrying your own food then make sure you have the lowest weight possible. For example, you should dispose of all food packaging before you depart as this will also rid you of all the litter you would then have to carry around as this is just dead weight. You should also aim to pack light-weight food that is easy to prepare as it will require fewer utensils to do so. If you are worried about a lack of flavour, it may be a good idea to carry small sachets of spices to make meals more exciting.

When it comes to snacks to eat on-the-go, cereal and muesli bars are great options. It is also nice to make your own trail mix. Simply purchase a bag of your favourite nuts, seeds, chocolate chips, and dried fruit and then place them into a small bag to keep on yourself for easy access and energy along the way. All of these can also be eaten separately depending on what resources you have, or that you can find along the way. Other options include rice cakes, chocolate bars, whole-grain tortillas, energy bars, chews or gels.

Again, when it comes to main meals remember to plan in advance. You should ensure that you are taking on a good mixture of complex and simple carbohydrates. For breakfast, porridge oats and wheat flakes with a bit of powdered milk mixed separately would be an ideal option. For dinner, noodles, pasta, and rice make safe, cheap, and light options although remember that rice can take a lot longer to cook. While dehydrated meals and boil in the bags are handy, they are often expensive and use both a lot of fuel and a lot of water. Of course, do not forget to pack instant coffee sachets for a refreshing cuppa to make your walk more enjoyable!

VILLAGE PUBS, SHOPS AND CAFES

As mentioned, you will pass through many towns and villages en route and they all offer a wide variety of local amenities such as pubs, cafes, and village shops. You will have many to choose from. Here you can stock up on supplies, or just have a generous meal in one of the pubs. At the start of each section, a number of selected facilities will be listed. Make sure that you account for the time spent in each place as well as the opening and closing time of aforementioned establishments.

The Double Locks

NAVIGATION

In the following section, you will find a list of maps you will require. Again, it is important to reiterate that The Two Counties Way is not a recognised trail but rather made up of traditional footpaths, that cut and weave through the countryside, country estates, farmsteads, and recognised trails. At the point from which you leave some of the other long-distance paths, there is little indication on which way the trail leads off, thus maps or prior knowledge of the route are essential.

Along the way, you will only encounter a few dedicated signs indicating you are heading in the right direction, notably upon reaching Tiverton and passing through Exeter. Otherwise, you will see the familiar Two Counties Way badge (listed on the next page) stapled to the more common footpath signposts, although these are infrequent and can become easily missed.

The scale of the map needed will depend on how much detail you wish to look at. Even though you can see footpaths on OS Landranger Mapping, OS Explorer maps tend to be more popular with walkers as they offer a greater detail of the terrain.

Remember, if you have a map at a scale of 1:25 000, every 1cm represents 25 000cm, in turn equalling to 250m in real life.

OS Explorer Maps, alternatively, are broken down into 4cm grid squares, with each grid square equalling 1km. Finally, OS Landranger Maps have 2cm grid squares equalling 1km.

MAPS COVERING THE ROUTE

OS Explorer Maps
1:25 000 Scale
4cm or 1 grid square = 1km

OS Landranger Maps
1:50 000 Scale
2cm or 1 grid square = 1km

OS xplorer 128
Taunton & Blackdown Hills

OS Landranger 193
Taunton & Lyme Regis, Chard &
Bridport

OS Explorer 114
Exeter & The Exe Valley

OS Landranger 181
Minehead & Brendon Hills

OS Explorer OL44
Torquay & Dawlish

OS Landranger 192
Exeter & Sidmouth

SIGNPOSTS & WAYMARKERS

Below are some of the examples that you will encounter and to keep a look out for.

KIT LIST

As with any expedition, planning is of paramount importance, thus compiling a suitable kit list of needed items is an essential task. Narrowing down the items that you need will ensure that you have a happier and safer experience. Depending on the type of outing that you have in mind, whether it be a country ramble, a backpacking holiday, or scaling the largest mountain ranges in the world, you are going to have to create a kit list specific to your expedition.

As mentioned, the Two Counties Way is roughly 56 miles long, however, it is up to you how long you take to reach the end of your trip. You need to think about how many hours or days you will spend completely each section and prepare your kit accordingly. Below I have provided a kit list that will give you some idea of the equipment that you might want to consider. This is a standard kit list of items that I often take with me on my walks. Of course, you should tailor it to your needs.

You can print this kit list out by visiting
(www.trailwanderer.co.uk/information/kit-list.pdf).

ON PERSON

Item	Notes	✓
Walking boots		
Walking trousers		
Map & Map cover		
Notebook and pen	Keep a note of accommodation on the route.	
Watch	Smart watch to log the route	
Beanie hat		
Buff		
Compass		
£50 / Wallet	Enough cash or transport or supplies.	

PERSONAL KIT CARRIED IN PACK

Item	Notes	✓
Waterproof Liner	A waterproof liner for the inside of the pack	
Sleeping bag		
Bivvy bag		
Roll mat		
Warm kit	Softie down jacket	
Spare socks	4 Pairs	
Spare underwear	4 Pairs	
Towel	Antibacterial towel	
Jet boil / Cooking system	Spare gas	
Hoochie / Tent	Tent pegs	
Bungees	5	
Hydration pack	2 litre	
Spare water	2 litre	
First aid kit	Plasters, deep heat, anti-fungal powder	
Food / Emergency rations	Noodles, boil in the bags, trail mix, nutrition bars	
Lighter/ matches	For lighting cooker	
Gloves		
Hand wipes	Antibacterial wipes	
Survival blanket		
Rubbish bag	For food packaging/general rubbish	

ADDITIONAL KIT

Item	Notes	✓
Spare batteries	3x AAA	
Spare laces		
Flip flops / Light weight trainers		
Portable charger		
Sun glasses		
Thermal mug		
Brew kit	Coffee / Tea sachets	
Multi-tool		
Walking poles		
Head torch		

Exeter Ship Canal

GETTING TO THE START POINT (TAUNTON)

BY RAIL

Taunton railway station is a stop on the main route that runs between London and Penzance. If arriving by rail you'll find the station located close to the town centre, approximately 1km from the main shopping area.

Upon arriving It's only a short walk to the start point. Leave the station and proceed out onto Station Road and turn left, follow along Station Road for about 700m until you reach 'The Bridge' also known as Tone Bridge. Take a right and proceed onto the footpath that runs between river's edge and the side of the building. Continue along the footpath until you enter out onto Clarence Street, from here turn left then after a few metres enter left into French Weir Park.

BY CAR

Taunton provides numerous car parking facilities that can be found in the town centre, however, Enfield car park is the closest to the starting point. Parking charges apply between the hours of 8 am – 6 pm Monday to Saturday. But, unless you plan on getting dropped off at the start point, you would need to consider if you would be happy with leaving your car in one sport for so long.

If you're coming from the North or South turn off at junction 25 from the M5 then take the 3rd exit onto the A358 and follow it around until arriving at the roundabout. From here, take the first exit onto Chritchard Way (A38). This proceeds all the way through into the town centre upon reaching the mini roundabout with the monument in the middle, again take the first left onto Corporation Street, then at the mini roundabout turn right onto Castle Street and follow it around to the left where the entrance to Enfield Car Park is located.

More information on car parking location and fees can be found by visiting **(www.tauntondeane.gov.uk/car-parks-parking/car-parks-in-taunton/).**

BUSES

Taunton's bus station can be found in the town centre, situated a short walk from Taunton Castle and The Museum of Somerset. The station acts as one of the popular stops for the National Express, so can easily be reached whether travelling from the north or south. Otherwise, if you are going to be travelling from the surrounding area or transferring via bus, then Taunton's bus station servers all the major towns and villages around Somerset.

To reach the start point from the bus station head right to the end of Tower Street then turn right onto Castle Street. Proceed along and take the next right onto Tangier Way and head over the bridge. Upon reaching the pedestrian crossing take the footpath leading right down to the footpath that runs alongside the River Tone. From here follow the footpath around, leading right, and on up to Clarence street, turn left and proceed straight to finally enter into French Weir Park on your left.

More information on bus services and routes can be found by visiting **(www.firstgroup.com/uploads/maps/network_map.pdf)**

LEAVING THE FINISHING POINT (STARCROSS)

BY RAIL

Starcross has a small single station platform. The route forms part of the scenic Riviera Line that provides an amazing coastal journey with alluring views of the southwest. Trains serve the station approximately every hour in both directions and normally run between Exmouth and Paignton via Exeter St Davids from where you can get onward connections to either the North or London. Or you can change at Newton Abbot continue down to Cornwall.

There are no facilities other than toilets and a shelter at the station so tickets will need to be purchased from the train conductor.

BY CAR

If you are looking at getting picked up from the finish point, getting to Starcross is quite simple. Come off at junction 30, signposted Dawlish A379. Head around the roundabout and take the 2nd exit onto the A379. Proceed straight and take the 3rd exit signposted Dawlish and enter along Rydon Lane. Head straight over at the roundabout onto Bridge Road and come off at the first exit at the next roundabout onto Sannerville Way (A379). Stay on this road passing through Kenton until eventually arriving at the train station. A car park can be found a short walk up from the station.

BUSES

If you find that getting home by bus would be more convenient, bus route number 2 is the main service that runs between Exeter and Newton Abbot from where you can get a connection. The route operates through the week from Monday to Sunday including bank holidays and is operated by Stagecoach Southwest. The main bus stop in Starcross is located next to the railway station.

DISTANCE CHART

Two Counties Way	Km	Miles	Elevation Gain
Taunton - Bradford on Tone	7	4.3	15m
Bradford on Tone - Wellington	5.8	3.6	35m
Wellington - Greenham	6	3.7	69m
Greenham - Sampford Peverell	8.5	5.2	29m
Sampford Peverell - Tiverton	12	7.4	72m
Tiverton - Bickleigh	6.3	3.9	81m
Bickleigh - Silverton	7.4	4.6	227m
Silverton - Broadclyst	8.6	5.4	88m
Broadclyst - Exeter (Quay)	12.8	8	192m
Exeter (Quay) - Starcross	17.1	10.6	87m
Total	**91.5km**	**56.8m**	**895m**

The mileage chart, pictured above, is useful to indicate the distance between each of the major settlements en route. As well as this, the chart also shows the expected elevation gain within each leg of the walk.

You will notice that for the most part the route is quite gentle and has very little elevation gain until you reach the steep hills that lie on the eastern side of the Exe valley onwards from Bickleigh, located in between the A396 and M5. Although steep, they are short in length.

HEIGHT ELEVATION

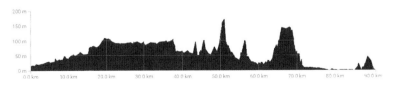

Please note: All figures given are approximations, these distances and elevation will vary based on diversions.

23

Rock Bridge, Grand Western Canal

THE ROUTE

Somerset

BRADFORD-ON-TONE

TAUNTON

GREENHAM

WELLINGTON

SAMPFORD PEVERELL

TIVERTON

BICKLEIGH

SILVERTON

BROADCLYST

EXETER

STARCROSS

LEG 1 - TAUNTON TO BRADFORD-ON-TONE

French Weir Park, Taunton

Taunton

OS Grid Ref: ST 2203 2481

District: Taunton Deane

OS Explorer map:

128 - Taunton & Blackdown Hills

Leg Distance: 7km / 4.3m

Elevation Gain: 15m

Points of interest

- Museum of Somerset
- Somerset Cricket Museum
- Vivary Park
- St James's Church
- St Mary Magdalene Church
- Taunton Visitor Centre

Accommodation & Eateries

- The Weir Café (Located at start point)
- Castle Hotel
- Taunton House Hotel
- Brookfield House B&B
- Beaufort Lodge B&B
- Lowdens House B&B

Bus Station

Main Bus Station

As of 2018, Taunton, the county town of Somerset, has a population of nearly 70,000 residents. Its name is derived from the fact it is a 'town on the River Tone'/ 'Tone Town' and it is fortunate enough to be filled with centuries of interesting military and religious history.

Within the heart of the town, for example, you will find Taunton Castle. The castle is thought to date back to the twelfth century and was built to defend the town; it has played an important role in the town through the centuries. In 1874, Somerset's Archaeological and Natural History Society bought the castle and today it is home to the Museum of Somerset with objects collected by the society on display within.

Another top attraction in the area is Vivary Park. Located a short walk from the town centre, Vivary Park has held the Taunton Flower Show ever since 1851. The park also offers the perfect place to picnic, relax, or to go for a stroll and take in the beautiful floral displays.

Rest assured, if you plan on stopping for a night in Taunton then there are plenty of hotels and B&Bs to choose from that are located all throughout the town.

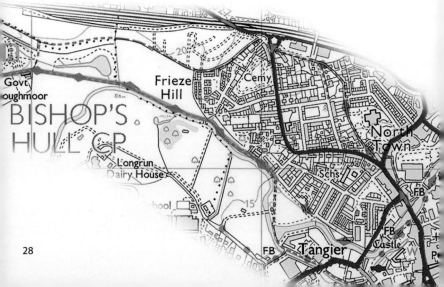

If you are ready to begin the trail, however, head to the French Weir Outdoor Activity Centre and Café. Start walking along the path up towards the north-west corner of the park; it is here that the trail begins.

The River Tone

The River Tone is approximately 21 miles (33km) in length. Its source can be found at Beaverton Pond in the Brendon Hills, within the boundaries of Exmoor National Park. It is dammed at Clatworthy Reservoir but the outflow continues onwards through Taunton and beyond, eventually joining up with the River Parrett.

After a few hundred metres continue to proceed straight passing the footbridge on your left. From here enter into the large field of Frieze Hill and head straight, again making sure you keep the river to your left. Once you reach the corner of this field you will briefly leave the river as it meanders on through Bishops Hull. You will meet up with it again slightly later though as it is never very far away from you on this section of the trail. Next, enter into the adjacent field and proceed straight. Keep to the gravel track and ensure the hedgerow is on your left and that the lake is on your right. When the gravel track bends round to the right, proceed straight onto the grassy trail. After a few metres, pass through a gate to enter onto the road and in front of a large building.

This road runs directly beside Taunton's Park & Ride, located in the west of the town. Upon arriving at the junction, turn left and follow the road.

Continue a short distance until you reach a gate on your right. This path leads into a small plantation with footpaths leading off in all directions. It is not overly clear which path to take but proceed straight ahead keeping the main plantation to your left. Upon reaching the right corner of the woodland, proceed into the adjacent field where you will have your first encounter with the remains of The Grand Western Canal. There is not much to see here though as it is now a dirt track used by tractors and walkers alike.

Again, continue straight heading to the corner of the field and enter into the next. Continue following the trail as it cuts directly across the middle of the next field.

When you reach the hedge line, bear diagonally left until you briefly meet up again with the River Tone. Follow the fence line until you pass the large warehouse on your left. Here, you reunite with the river once more and should continue alongside it until you reach a road that runs through to the village of Allerford.

Head straight over the road and into the next field. Here, you can either cut diagonally across to join at the bend in the river or proceed directly alongside the river. In any case, it is hard to go wrong as the path continues alongside, or close to, the river's edge crossing through numerous fields and over various footbridges. Take note that with the path being so close to the river, and the amount of rainfall we normally experience in the UK, this section does tend to become extremely muddy, especially in the winter months.

Upon reaching a large weir over to your left, it is then only a short distance along the river until you reach the rather small but medieval Bradford Bridge, located to the north-west of the first village that you encountered on the trail. Head over the bridge, leaving behind the West Deane Way trail, and follow the path into the village of Bradford-on-Tone. Now is the time take a rest stop and pick up any needed supplies you may have forgotten.

Bradford Bridge

Bradford Bridge is a double arched span bridge made out of stone. It is said to have been built by monks, although it is not known which group of monks carried out the work.

The bridge is believed to have been built sometime between the thirteenth and fifteenth century, as such, it has been designated a Grade II listed building and scheduled as an ancient monument. Fortunately, despite several restoration phases over many centuries, the bridge still retains much of its natural features and form.

Grid Ref:
ST 171 229

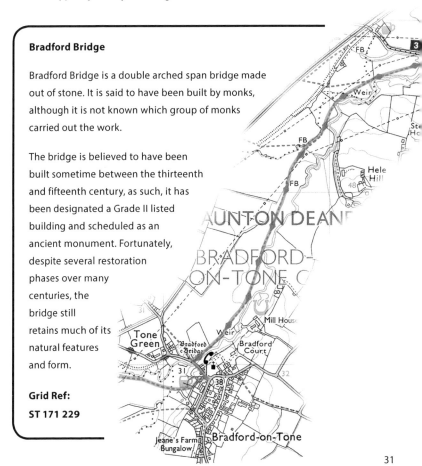

Heading out to Silk Mills Road

Leading up to Bradford-on-Tone

LEG 2 - BRADFORD-ON-TONE TO WELLINGTON

St Giles' Church, Bradford-on-Tone

Bradford-on-Tone

OS Grid Ref: ST 1737 2286

District: Taunton Deane

OS Explorer map:

128 - Taunton & Blackdown Hills

Leg Distance: 5.8km / 3.6m

Elevation Gain: 35m

Points of interest

- St Giles Church
- Village Hall

Accommodation & Eateries

- Bradford-on-Tone Village Shop
- The White Horse Inn

The name Bradford is distinctly English thus the villages name 'Bradford-on-Tone' is no accident. In fact, Bradford-on-Tone has stood since the days of the Saxons. Home to roughly 662 residents, this village is situated directly beneath the River Tone and approximately 4 miles (6.4 km) south-west of Taunton.

Bradford-on-Tone is home to few facilities. You will find the local village shop tucked away in the building behind the red telephone box, situated next to The White Horse Inn. The village shop is maintained entirely by volunteers and is run on a "not-for-profit" basis for the benefit of the local community and anyone who happens to be passing through. It is open every morning from 9 am until 12 pm should you need to acquire any supplies, although items on offer are limited.

The White Horse Inn itself dates back to the sixteenth century and provides traditional pub food. That said, it is best to double-check opening times ahead if you plan on stopping here for a meal as these cannot always be guaranteed.

Another point of interest to note is the large church of St Giles. Dating back to the thirteenth century, St Giles is lucky enough to retain much of the characteristics and design unique to that era. It is also thought to stand on the site of a former wooden Saxon church.

To proceed on with the walk, begin at the telephone box in front of the village shop. First, head around the right-hand side of the box and head into the carpark of the White Horse Inn. Proceed to the right-hand corner of the carpark and follow the walkway down to a gate and on into a field. From here follow the path down through the fields and cross over the footbridge to the opposite side of the River Tone. Next, follow the path leading to the left and enter through into the next field. Proceed along until you have crossed the pedestrian railway level crossing. Take care crossing over the railway track as it is a very busy line; it is the main line to run between Cornwall and London as well as to the North of England.

Once over, head down to the river once again and you will soon reach a weir. Follow the path along and down the side of Clavenges Farm. Eventually, join up with the road that runs on up into East Nynehead. At the road, turn right onto it and proceed past the large house on your right. Just after this house, but before the next brick barn building, head over the stile and into the meadow on your left.

Continue onwards across into another field until you enter out onto the road that runs horizontally through East Nynehead. Here, you will join up with the West Deane Way again.

Turn left and head a short distance until you come to a driveway on your left that proceeds down to Perry Farm. Carry on down the driveway, and, upon reaching the bend, pass through the gate into the field on your right.

Now proceed to the bottom right of the field, either by following the hedge line around to your right or by cutting diagonally across. When you reach the corner, turn right and follow alongside the next hedge line of the adjacent field. Venture past the small water treatment works building and follow the hedge along as it bends around to the left.

The Nynehead Lift

An engineer named James Green first built the Nynehead lift in the 1830s. The whole idea of the lift was to provide a solution for overcoming a steep accent within a short distance. The lifts worked by using caissons filled with water combined with the principle of displacement. Such lifts were among the first in the country to be commercially successful and they operated for 30 years up until the Canal was closed by the Exeter & Railway Company in 1865. After this date, all the machinery was removed.

In total there were seven lifts along the Grand Western Canal. Today, though all were removed, there are still substantial remains of the Nynehead Lift that are visible. An original detailed description of operation and drawings also still exist.

Grid Ref: ST 144 218

Here you will be greeted with a bridge that crosses the River Tone. This marks the first real detectable remnants of the Grand Western Canal. Continue over the bridge following the track along the hedge line until you enter out by the side of a house and onto Nynehead Road. Turn left and then directly right through the gate before proceeding into a narrow walkway that leads through Blackham Copse. You will see that the trail leads alongside a gravel road; this road that used to form part of the canal. Continue onwards until you reach the stone ruins of the Nynehead Lift.

Climb the steps to the left of the ruins and enjoy the view of the ruins from up top before turning left. Proceed leading away from the lift and into Long Copse woodland. Here, you will again be brought fairly close to the railway line but the path will then bend round to the right. Even though this section is littered with trees you are still able to distinguish the former channel of the canal.

Upon leaving the woodland, enter out into a clearing. From here, you will be able to see the industrial estate and chimney stack of Tonedale as well as the aforementioned site of the former Tonedale Mill. Proceed down alongside the hedgerow and head towards the left-hand side of the sewage treatment works. Follow the track past the works to finally enter out onto the Milverton Road (B3187). You are now in Tone, north-west of Wellington.

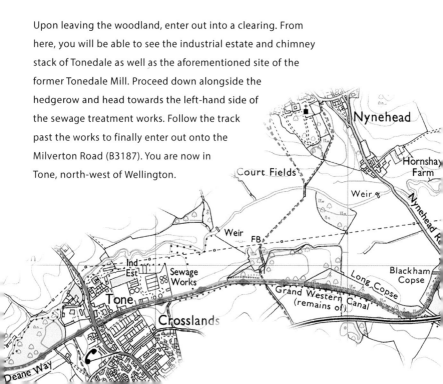

LEG 3 - WELLINGTON TO GREENHAM

Wellington Park, Wellington

Wellington

OS Grid Ref: ST 1262 2190

District: Taunton Deane

OS Explorer map:
128 - Taunton & Blackdown Hills

Leg Distance: 6 km / 3.7 miles

Elevation Gain: 69m

Points of interest

- Tourist Information

Accommodation & Eateries

- Convenience shop located nearby (appx 500m).
- Main shops and cafes are located in town centre (appx 1.8km). Runnington Cider Barn B&B

Buses

22, 22A - Taunton to Tiverton

Wellington is a small town located 7 miles south-west of Taunton. Close to the border of Devon, around 14,500 residents live in Wellington; this figure includes the villages of Tone and Tonedale. Consequently, there are many local amenities to be found in the town centre.

It is important to note that Wellington's town centre is some distance away at roughly 1.8 km from where you enter out into Tone. Do not forget account for this added distance should you wish to take a look around the centre and take in the shops.

If you are not feeling up to the walk into town, and you are running low on supplies, you can find a local convenience store approximately 500m along Station Road that leads into Wellington.

There is not much to be found within Tone other than industrial buildings. However, the area used to play a very important role in Britain's woollen history as the area was home to the largest woollen mill complex in the south-west. All of which have long since vanished but you can still see the remains of the buildings and chimney stacks of both the Tone Mill and Tonedale Mill which is located just south of Tone.

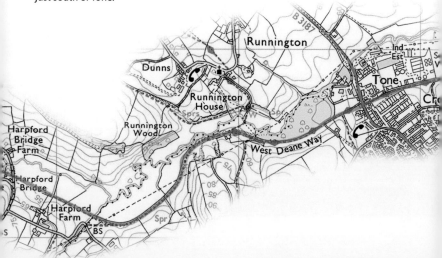

Tonedale and Tone Mills

Both Tonedale Mills and Tone Mills were large woollen factories and most famously produced the khaki dye used by the British Army. The sites were notable for having each type of power generation in that of water, steam and electricity.

The woollen industry thrived in the 1700s and the site continued to grow into well into the nineteenth century, where at its peak, it employed around 3,600 employees. Sadly, by the 1980s the complex was vastly downsized due to the cheaper cost of producing fabric abroad. Most parts remain abandoned or have been sold off to developers, apart from a small-scale production unit.

From where you entered out onto Milverton Road, cross over the road and look for the sign directing you down a trackway that runs to the side of a house.

A short distance past the house, enter through a gate into a field. From here, the path leads along the base of a hill. And around a dense patch of woodland before curving around to the right.

Next, proceed into the following field. You should be able to see raised grassy mounds that once carried the towpath that ran alongside the canal. Continue following the channel. From here, you will leave the West Deane Way as it heads up on into the village of Langford Budville, through Runnington.

Keep following along what once would have been the canal next to the base of the hills until you arrive at Harpford Farm. Pass by the north side and head on over to Harpford Bridge. Proceed underneath and into the grounds of the building located on the left. Pass over the stream, up the steps, and over the stile into the field.

Here, you will glimpse a short section of a canal-shaped lake, which now forms part of the Rewe Mead Nature Reserve that sits on the river bank of the River Tone.

Head along the right-hand side of the former canal as the trail leads along the underside of the river. Once through two more sections of the reserve look out for a signpost pointing left and head towards the corner.

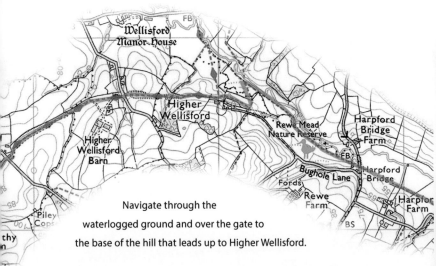

Navigate through the waterlogged ground and over the gate to the base of the hill that leads up to Higher Wellisford.

Head up the hillside until you are level with the fence that forms the boundary of the farm. Continue straight and follow the hedgerow, keeping it on your left at all times. Continue through numerous other fields. Try to keep to the high ground as the remains of the canal are likely to be waterlogged. Eventually, you will enter out onto a country lane that runs down into Thorne St Margaret.

Upon arriving at the road, take the turning over to the left and the drive leading up to Thornemead Farm. Once halfway up the drive, take the path leading off to the treeline to the right. From here, follow the path alongside the tree line all the way up to Cothay Bridge Farm. Enter out onto the road and follow the driveway out onto Piley Lane. At the junction, proceed straight ahead and bypass the entrance of the drive that leads to Cothay Manor on your right.

At the bend, proceed up the driveway of Elworthy Farm. Upon reaching the barn, head around the left-hand side and into the field located behind. Proceed over to the right-hand side and follow the walkway through several other fields to finally enter out on to Bishop's Hill, a road that runs through the village of Greenham.

LEG 4 - GREENHAM TO SAMPFORD PEVERELL

Bishop's Hill, Greenham

Greenham

OS Grid Ref: ST 0782 2023

District: Taunton Deane

OS Explorer map:
128 - Taunton & Blackdown Hills

Leg Distance: 8.5 km / 5.2 miles

Elevation Gain: 29m

Points of interest

- St Peter's Church

Accommodation & Eateries

- Greenham Hall
- Beambridge Inn
- The Old Dairy B&B
- Gamlins Farm Caravan Park
- The Globe Inn
  (located in Appley appx 1.8km)

The hamlet of Greenham also sits on the banks of the meandering River Tone. Located within Stawley parish, it shares this parish with the villages of Stawley and Kittsford, as well as a collection of hamlets, including Appley and Tracebridge.

Although you will not find any facilities at the start of this leg, you can find The Globe Inn located roughly 1.8 km away in Appley. If you plan on camping around here, you can find Gamlins Farm Caravan Park 800m south of Greenham.

Greenham is home, however, to two historic houses that can be found within the close vicinity of each other: Greenham Hall and Greenham Barton. Another point of interest may be St Peter's Church.

Solicitor Thomas Edward Clarke had the Greenham Hall Country House built in 1848. Admiral Sir J D Kelly, however, later bought the house from him. Today it now serves as a B&B where you can enjoy a peaceful night's rest and even explore the garden's large collection of perennials if you so wish.

Nearby, you can also visit another manor house named Greenham Barton. Originally built in the thirteenth century, it is a Grade I listed building and is a wonderful site to behold.

To continue with the walk, following on from the opening that you entered out onto Bishop's Hill, turn left and look out for the stile a short distance along and over to your right-hand side.

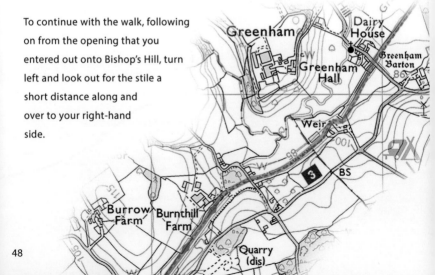

Cross over the stile and head along the narrow track leading towards the farm buildings. Next, cross over the drive and head around the left side of the large barn. Once into the next field, proceed along the hedge line until you enter on to a country lane. Head straight up the road directly in front until you come upon Lowdwells Lock, located at the edge of the Somerset / Devon border.

You are now at the Eastern end of the remaining intact Grand Western Canal; it is from this point onwards that remains open today and runs the whole eleven miles into Tiverton. At this point, you will find a bench located just over to the left of the start point. This bench offers an excellent respite before commencing the eight kilometers to reach Sampford Peverell.

From here it is difficult to go wrong as it is a case of following the towpath that runs alongside the canal through and into Tiverton. On the right-hand side, the trail initially starts out as a wide gravel path until it slightly narrows into a dirt track as it runs down to the road of Dunn's Hill, the first bridge that crosses over the canal.

Upon reaching the bridge you may notice the very small and claustrophobic Waytown Tunnel down to your left that once allowed barges to pass beneath the bridge.

49

After crossing the bridge to the opposite side, proceed down and along the left-hand side of the canal. After a short distance, on the opposite side of the canal, you will notice more ruins from old industry in the form of the Waytown Lime Kilns.

The Waytown Lime Kilns

Back in the nineteenth century, lime was mainly used for improving the soil for agricultural land. The calcium contained within lime is essential for plant growth as it neutralises acidity.

It is thought the lime kilns were built sometime between 1810 and 1814. Limestone was quarried above the canal then transported by pack horse to the kilns. It is interesting to note that local red limestone is in fact still quarried at Westleigh Quarry. Anyway, initially the Waytown Lime Kilns were built with three kilns, the large arches being the kilns and the smaller arches providing shelter for workers drawing the lime. It is not known when the kilns were last fired up but today you will instead find nesting jackdaws who have taken up residence in this derelict area.

Grid Ref: ST 070 189

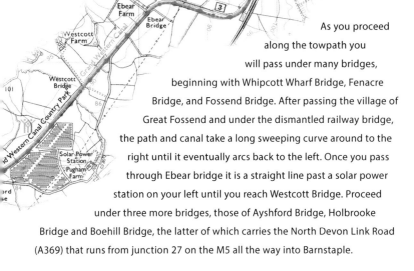

As you proceed along the towpath you will pass under many bridges, beginning with Whipcott Wharf Bridge, Fenacre Bridge, and Fossend Bridge. After passing the village of Great Fossend and under the dismantled railway bridge, the path and canal take a long sweeping curve around to the right until it eventually arcs back to the left. Once you pass through Ebear bridge it is a straight line past a solar power station on your left until you reach Westcott Bridge. Proceed under three more bridges, those of Ayshford Bridge, Holbrooke Bridge and Boehill Bridge, the latter of which carries the North Devon Link Road (A369) that runs from junction 27 on the M5 all the way into Barnstaple.

After arriving at the far side of Boehill Bridge there is a footpath that leads down in the direction of Tiverton Parkway rail station, roughly 1km. Should you wish to retire from the trail at this point, this provides a perfect opportunity to do so.

Otherwise, proceed onwards along the towpath. After passing under the final bridge, named Buckland Bridge, you will enter into the centre of Sampford Peverell behind the sports pitches and public car park.

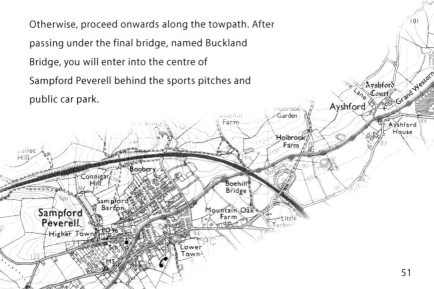

LEG 5 - SAMPFORD PEVERELL TO TIVERTON

Lower Town Road, Sampford Peverell

Sampford Peverell

OS Grid Ref: ST 0285 1429

District: Mid Devon

OS Explorer map:
114 - Exeter & the Exe Valley

Leg Distance: 12 km / 7.4 miles

Elevation Gain: 72m

Points of interest

- Sampford Peverell Village Hall
- St John the Baptist Church

Accommodation & Eateries

- Convenience Store
- The Globe Inn
- The Merriemeade
- Your Plaice or Mine (Friday 5pm - 8pm)

Buses

1, 1A, 1B - Tiverton to Exeter via
Cullompton

The pretty village of Sampford Peverell, home to around 1,300 people, sits just west of junction 27 of the M5. The name of the village reflects its inclusion in the Honour of Peverell where geographical areas of England were granted to the Peverell family by William the Conqueror several decades ago.

The Grand Western Canal runs directly through the centre of the village but you can find the village facilities from the main road. These can be reached by cutting along the footpath that runs next to the side of the sports pitches or by entering into The Globe Inn car park. Other facilities include a post office, farm shop, another pub named The Merriemeade, and a mobile fish and chip shop that can be found along the main road near to the sports pitches. Please note, all of these only open on selected days.

If you decided to stop and take a look around Sampford Peverell you can make your way back to the canal either through the car park of the Globe Inn, or, if you proceed along the road that runs through Sampford Peverell, Lower Town Road, you can then merge left into Chains Road which leads down to the canal towpath.

Upon finally re-joining the towpath continue left making your way, firstly, towards Battens Bridge. Shortly after, the path takes a wide curve around to the right before you eventually arrive at Rock Bridge. Pass underneath and continue to follow the path around to the left.

Embankment collapse

In 2012, this section of the canal's 60 ft. 200-year-old clay bank gave way due to a torrent of severe weather and heavy rain. The breach sent millions of gallons of water pouring down the hillside. Repairs were carried out and workers rebuilt the failed embankment. The canal was also lined with an impermeable material along the length of the section. On the 24th March 2014, officials reopened the canal once again.

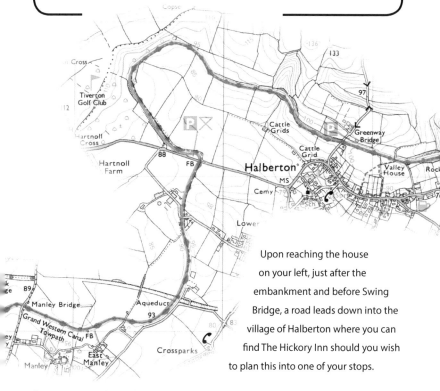

Upon reaching the house on your left, just after the embankment and before Swing Bridge, a road leads down into the village of Halberton where you can find The Hickory Inn should you wish to plan this into one of your stops.

If not, continue along the towpath heading under Greenway Bridge and Swing Bridge. From here on, you can take in the with delightful views as well as the

tranquillity
and peacefulness
of the surrounding area and

back towards Halberton. Here, the canal also takes a sweep out on a large arcing loop, called the Swan's Neck'. It almost comes back on itself before arriving next to Tiverton Road car park, a parking area for members of the public.

Here, located next to the car park, you will find the Dudley Weatherley lift bridge built in 2002 to commemorate the Queen's fiftieth jubilee. It is kindly named after

---

Canberra Bomber Crash

On the 21st November 1961, an RAF Canberra bomber, crewed by pilot Flight Lieutenant Roger Johnson Moore, and Navigator Flying Officer Martin James Edward Archard, took off from RAF Geilenkirchen in Germany. They made their way on a high-low navigation training flight via Devon.

Whilst flying over Tiverton, the pilot radioed in to report an engine fault. The plane was seen by locals turning away before crashing into the canal. Sadly, both crew members died. It is believed that by staying with the plane they saved many lives on the ground. In the weeks that followed, services managed to recover both their bodies and the plane's wreckage.

It was only in 2003 when contractors were employed to dredge a section of the canal that the silt they were removing smelt strongly of fuel. When they came across large pieces of metal around Manley Bridge, the story of the crash emerged again and plans were set in motion to establish a memorial for the two servicemen who lost their lives.

a well-known artist who became prominent in the campaign to save the canal, back in the 1960s and 1970s.

Keeping to the towpath, and upon reaching Crownhill Bridge (also suitably known as Change path), cross over the bridge to the other side. A little further on, cross over the Aqueduct. Originally built in 1847, the Tiverton Parkway to Tiverton branch used to run underneath; two arches were built for two lines but only one was ever used. It was eventually closed in 1967.

Finally, pass under both East Manley and Manley bridge before commencing the last mile of the route as it passes through the southern residential area of Tiverton before finally arriving at the Tiverton Canal Basin where you can find a visitors area and selection of cafes.

Here, you will also find the most unique experience of this walk. You can take a two and a half hour round trip on one of the last remaining horse-drawn barges in the UK. It does, however, operate on a timetable and it only runs certain times of the year. Be sure to check it out online prior to arriving in order to avoid missing out.

LEG 6 - TIVERTON TO BICKLEIGH

Memorial Hall, Tiverton

Tiverton

OS Grid Ref: SS 9541 1249

District: Mid Devon

OS Explorer map:
114 - Exeter & the Exe Valley

Leg Distance: 6.3 km / 3.9 miles

Elevation Gain: 81m

Points of interest

- Tiverton Canal Co
- Tiverton Castle
- Tiverton Museum of Mid Devon Life

Accommodation & Eateries

- Ducks Ditty café
- Elsie May's Café
- Mad Hatters Café
- The Frying Pickle
- Best Western Hotel
- The Twyford Hotel
- Tiverton Hotel

Buses

1, 1A, 1B - Tiverton to Exeter via
            Cullompton
55, 55A, 55B - Tiverton to Exeter
155 - Barnstaple to Exeter via Tiverton

Tiverton, with a population of approximately 19,500 residents, lies just to the north of Exeter. The town is fortunate to be steeped in history; evidence of human occupation dates back to the stone age and many artefacts such as flint tools have been found in the area. You will even find an Iron Age hill fort named Cranmore Castle that stands on top of the towering Exeter Hill.

Tiverton is a fairly large town for the area so you can expect to find plenty of amenities in the form of pubs, restaurants, and cafes. There are also several B&Bs, should you wish to plan in a stopover in the town.

One notable point of interest in the area is Tiverton Castle. First built in 1106, this castle, like many fortified manors in the area, played a small part in the English Civil War. Royalists initially held the castle before a brief siege led parliamentarians to take over. Further, located just outside of Tiverton is a Grade I listed Victorian country house titled Knightshayes Court and Gardens. It is now operated and owned by the National Trust should you wish to visit.

Tiverton Castle

Tiverton Castle sits just up from the main high street and occupies a defensive position above the banks of the River Exe. Originally it started out as a Norman Motte-and-bailey castle that was built in 1106. Throughout the twelfth and thirteenth centuries, it was then altered and extended. Later on, during the Civil War, the castle provided a stronghold for the Royalists until Parliamentarian troops set siege to the castle and very luckily hit one of the chains holding up the drawbridge. This allowed a group of roundheads to rush in and end the siege. Soon after the defensive structure of the castle was demolished to prevent any other military use of the castle.

After the war ended it was converted into a country house. It remains this way today and is open to the public for tours. If you time it right you can even stay in one of the three large properties that make up the castle – how about that for a restful night's sleep.

If you are keen to find out more about the history of local rural life, you can further visit Tiverton Museum of Mid Devon Life, located next to the bus station.

From here on the trail takes on a rather different type of backdrop as you leave the relatively flat towpath of the Grand Western Canal behind. On this section of the route, you will proceed down and over the eastern side of the Exe valley. As you can probably see right now by looking at Exeter Hill, you will encounter several more of these steep rolling hills on your journey. Overall though some of the hills that you will ascend will be steep they will usually be short and the views that await you are well worth the effort.

To continue the Two Counties Way, leave the Grand Western Canal Country Park and enter out onto Canal Hill. Turn right and descend down the hill. At the base, just before the bend, turn left onto Deyman's Hill and proceed straight ahead. Upon reaching the next bend follow straight along the small dirt track that leads down and enters out onto Tumbling Field Lane. It is at this point that you join up onto yet another long-distance walking trail, the Exe Valley Way. Traditionally, this route starts in Starcross and proceeds up the Exe Valley and across Exmoor to finally finish in Exford, a total distance of 52 miles.

At the junction where you join onto Tumbling Fields, turn left and follow the road around before taking the left onto Collipriest Road. Proceed along Collipriest Road as it bends around to the right. The road will then join up with the River Exe for a few hundred meters until the road bends off to the left, away from the River Exe.

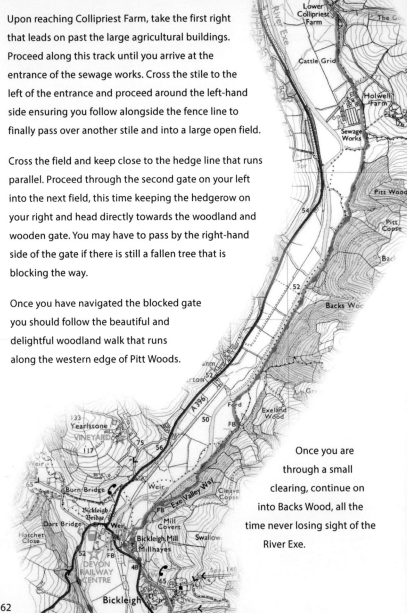

Upon reaching Collipriest Farm, take the first right that leads on past the large agricultural buildings. Proceed along this track until you arrive at the entrance of the sewage works. Cross the stile to the left of the entrance and proceed around the left-hand side ensuring you follow alongside the fence line to finally pass over another stile and into a large open field.

Cross the field and keep close to the hedge line that runs parallel. Proceed through the second gate on your left into the next field, this time keeping the hedgerow on your right and head directly towards the woodland and wooden gate. You may have to pass by the right-hand side of the gate if there is still a fallen tree that is blocking the way.

Once you have navigated the blocked gate you should follow the beautiful and delightful woodland walk that runs along the western edge of Pitt Woods.

Once you are through a small clearing, continue on into Backs Wood, all the time never losing sight of the River Exe.

Once you arrive at a very large clearing, an area popular with dog walkers, you can either cut straight across towards the top left corner of the field, or, if it takes your fancy, you can take a more leisurely and relaxing stroll alongside the river as it bends slightly out and around to end up at the same top left corner.

At the corner of the field enter through the gate and cross over the small footbridge. From here, you should join back up to another large patch of woodland where you will proceed onwards and down through the final gate that leads to the back end of Bickley Mill.

Bickleigh Mill

LEG 7 - BICKLEIGH TO SILVERTON

Bickleigh Bridge, Bickleigh

Bickleigh

OS Grid Ref: SS 9406 0720

District: Mid Devon

OS Explorer map:

114 - Exeter & the Exe Valley

Leg Distance: 7.4 km / 4.6 miles

Elevation Gain: 227m

Points of interest

- Bickleigh Bridge
- Bickleigh Castle
- Devon Railway Centre
- St Mary The Virgin Church
- Saint Mary's Church

Accommodation & Eateries

- Bickleigh Mill
- The Trout Inn
- Fisherman's Cot Pub
- Yearlstone Vineyard Cafe
- Lodgehill Hotel

Buses

155, 55, 55A - Tiverton to Exeter

Bickleigh, with an approximate population of about 239 residents, is located four miles south of Tiverton. It is quite a beautiful and idyllic country village with numerous thatched cottages to admire along the way.

Entering out into the carpark of the historic eighteenth century Bickleigh Mill, you will be located just down from Bickleigh's Village Centre. From this point, you can visit some of the notable points of interests in the area and take in some of Bickleigh's facilities. Firstly, Bickleigh Mill itself provides bistro dining along with rural shopping. Additionally, located just next door to the Mill is the ever popular Devon Railway Centre with an adjoining tea room.

Should you desire a pub lunch, you have the choice of either the Fisherman's Cot or The Trout Inn. Both can be reached by passing over the village's medieval bridge. This bridge forms part of the A396, the road running between Tiverton and Exeter.

Within the vicinity of both pubs, you can also find Bickleigh castle manor house which now serves as a B&B. Alternatively, to the north, up on the hillside above The Trout Inn, you can find Yearlstone Vineyard, one of the largest vineyards in the Southwest.

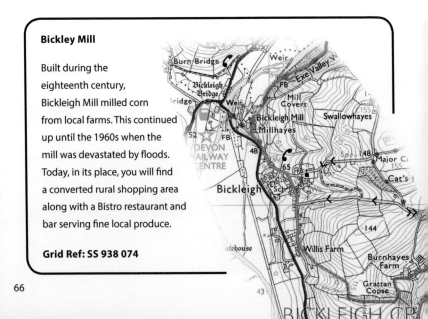

Bickley Mill

Built during the eighteenth century, Bickleigh Mill milled corn from local farms. This continued up until the 1960s when the mill was devastated by floods. Today, in its place, you will find a converted rural shopping area along with a Bistro restaurant and bar serving fine local produce.

Grid Ref: SS 938 074

Bickleigh Castle

Set in 60 acres of land, Bickleigh Castle stands on the banks of the River Exe. The castle is now comprised of a group of buildings from different periods but was once considerably larger. Like many manors of the area, it also played a role during the English Civil War. Charles I's queen Henrietta Maria, for example, stayed in the castle whilst on her way to Exeter. A year later, towards the end of 1645, Parliamentarian troops eventually attacked the castle and destroyed the main building.

Grid Ref: SS 936 068

To continue with the route, start at Bickleigh Mill's car park. Head left and out onto the A369. Next, take the first left that leads on into the village and pass St Mary's Church on your right. Proceed up the hill and then take the second right. Continue along this road until you reach a thatched white cottage on your right. To your left, you will see a pathway leading up to a gate.

Enter through the gate and onwards through the two sets of metal gates at each end of the stables. Once into the field, you will encounter the first strenuous part of the entire route. It might be a bit of a slog at first but press on up the hill and head towards the stile half way up. This is a good place to catch your breath and take in the spectacular views looking back over to the west hills of the Exe Valley.

From the stile, it is a brief downhill section before again pursuing another steep uphill climb. Upon reaching the top of the hill, proceed right and over to the stile next to Grattan Copse. Be careful here as it can become quite windy owing to the exposed position you are in.

Once over the stile, turn left and head to the very end of the copse. Turn left again and head down until you reach the next stile and cross back over into the adjacent field and follow the path around. At the end, turn right and down into Burnhayes Farm. The trail leads straight through the centre of the farm so take care and watch out for farm animals. Once out on the drive, head on down to the main road that runs alongside the Burn River.

At the end of the drive turn right and carry along the road for roughly 1km until you come across a footpath signpost pointing left. Cut over the small footbridge and proceed between the buildings. Turn right and follow the road up.

Next, take the first left. This road bends back around to the right and presents another strenuous and steep section of the route. However, once at the top of the hill, bear right and proceed along the ridgeline; pass through Ravenhayes.

After the sharp 90 degree left bend in the road, take a left turn up Coombe Lane. Stick to the lane until you reach a sign post pointing through the large metal gate.

Head in the direction of the signpost and follow along the track passing below Coblands Farm. At the second signpost turn right. Head on through the gate and you will arrive at the base of a hill. Proceed over to the hedgeline that runs up the right-hand side of the field and press on up the hill.

Continue uphill until you pass Coblands Farm. Keeping a look out for a turn on your right. From here you will be quite high up above the farm; the views offered looking back up the Exe valley are quite spectacular, even better on a clear sunny day!

Proceed along the edge of the field until reaching the next one. From here, head uphill towards the left-hand side where you will encounter a stile that takes you into the next meadow. Once over, continue diagonally and head towards the far-left corner. Enter the next field and stick to the wide dirt track that runs along the side of it.

You will now be located at the brow of the hill. Directly in front of you will be a wind turbine. As you approach the turbine, and come to the summit of the 195 m hill, you should be in for a real treat as this has to be the most breath-taking vantage point of the entire 56-mile trail. You will be located directly above Silverton. If the weather conditions are good, you should have panoramic views stretching for miles. You can see the Exe Estuary towards Exmouth as well as the finishing point. Further, you should be able to see the rising hills of Dartmoor over to the south west, and even the grounds of Killerton Garden's and Broadclyst where the Two Counties Way continues onwards next.

From the hill summit, the trail down to Silverton is quite visible and is fortunately marked by signposts. Head around to the right of the hedgerow directly in front and proceed down through the gate into the next field. From here, cut directly across the middle and on into the next. When you catch sight of the farm building at the base of the hill, bear left and head towards the lower left of the field. Crossover the gate and enter the drive way that leads out Silverdale Road.

At the road turn left then immediately right and onto the High Street. From here, follow along the road all the way into the centre of Silverton where you will find the village centre.

LEG 8 - SILVERTON TO BROADCLYST

School Road, Silverton

Silverton

OS Grid Ref: SS 9555 0286

District: Mid Devon

OS Explorer map:

114 - Exeter & the Exe Valley

Leg Distance: 8.6 km / 5.4 miles

Elevation Gain: 88m

Points of interest

- St Mary The Virgin Church
- Silverton Community Hall

Accommodation & Eateries

- Convenience Store
- Butchers
- The Lamb Inn
- The Silverton Inn
- Newcourt Barn Self Catering

Buses

55A, 55B - Tiverton to Exeter

Silverton is a large village situated eight miles to the north of Exeter. It is one of the oldest villages in Devon as it dates back to the first year of the Saxon occupations.

In Silverton, you will find a few facilities that are easily located from the mini roundabout within the village centre. Should you require any supplies, there is a convenience store next to the butchers. You can also find The Silverton Inn and the Lamb Inn along Fore Street. If you plan on using Silverton as a stop off you can find local B&Bs online and can even stay at The Silverton Inn.

St Mary: The Virgin Church provides another notable point of interest along this route. The building dates back to the fifteenth or sixteenth century and is a beautiful site to visit for those interested in architecture or religion.

To continue the Two Counties Way, from the mini roundabout located in the centre of Silverton head in the opposite direction of Fore Street, along Newcourt Road and pass the shops on your right. After the second left but before Channons Farm, take the next left onto a bridleway that runs up and rejoins onto the road leading out of Silverton. At the bend of the bridal way, turn right and at the fork, take a left turn.

Upon reaching the crossroads, head straight over onto Hayne Lane and proceed down keeping Hayne House on your left. Upon reaching the end of the lane, head straight along the farm track. After a short distance, bear right into a narrow walkway that runs along the edge of a field.

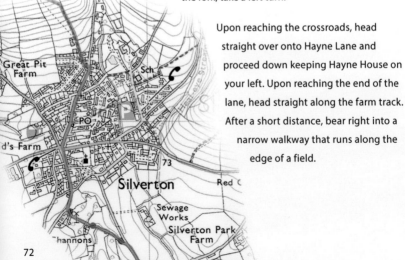

Pass through the gate and proceed to the pedestrian railway crossing that can be found at the top left corner of the field. The path is clearly marked by the flatten grass.

Take care when crossing over the rail tracks then follow the path that runs close to the River Culm and head towards the gate that is located on the left-hand side of the Ellerhayes Bridge. Enter out onto the road, cross over the bridge, and turn right into the carpark.

From this point, you will be entering on to the beautiful grounds of Killerton. It is important to note that the paths through the woodland can become a bit of a maze as there are several paths leading off in all directions, therefore it can become quite disorientating. However, if you do happen to get lost there are a number of signposts directing you back to the house. If all else fails, look at making your way to Killerton House where you can pick up the trail again.

Enter through the gate of the car park and proceed up the gravel track as this leads up and around the perimeter and into the woods. When you arrive at the first obvious fork, turn left and head upwards deeper into Park Wood. Continue straight, taking the next left and continue onwards. The path eventually loops around to the left before coming back round to meet up with other footpaths.

At the crossroads, head straight and continue along the edge of the boundary of the woods. After reaching the end of a clump of trees go left and proceed straight, heading past the south side of Killerton House. This path runs parallel to the road that leads from the house out to the main road. As you pass Killerton Stables on your left, towards the entrance you can find the National Trust run café and souvenir shop.

Killerton House and Gardens

Covering some 2,590 hectares, Sir Thomas Acland built Killerton House in the eighteenth century. The National Trust then bought the building in 1994 and it remains owned by them today. The grounds of this estate offer some beautiful walks, its gardens and these walks are listed on the National Register of Historic Parks & Gardens. There is also a steep wooded hillside where the remains of an Iron hill fort can be found at the top.

Upon reaching the road, turn right then take the next left as it leads along and down to Francis Court Farm. Once at the farm, proceed up the concrete sleeper track that leads up and in-between two fields.

At the hedgerow, take a direct right and follow the hedge downwards until you meet up with the M5. Proceed over the footbridge and on into the next field. From here, keep to the fence on your left and proceed straight up and over the stile until you finally come level with Reed's Cottages. This serves as a high point and you will be able to spot the tower of Broadclyst's St John the Baptist's Church in the short distance.

From the cottages, head downhill and across another meadow until you pass Mooredge Farm then through the middle of Martinsfield Farm. Upon reaching Martinsfield Farm, head through the gate directly in front and follow the track straight.

Next, follow the track round to the right before curving round to the left. After the left turn, head on up to finally arrive at the side of the Red Lion Inn located in village of Broadclyst.

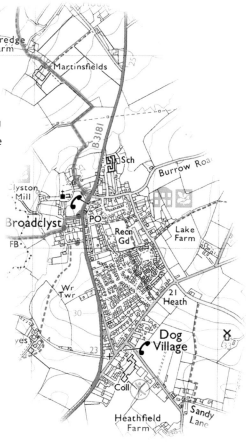

LEG 9 - BROADCLYST TO EXETER (QUAY)

B3181, Broadclyst

Broadclyst

OS Grid Ref: SX 9826 9717

District: East Devon

OS Explorer map:

114 - Exeter & the Exe Valley

Leg Distance: 12.8 km / 8 miles

Elevation Gain: 192m

Points of interest

- St John the Baptist Church
- National Trust, Clyston Mill
- National Trust, Maker's Cottage
- Victory Hall
- Post Office

Accommodation & Eateries

- The Red Lion
- Spice & Stone
- Jarvis Hayes B&B
- Hues Piece Paynes Farm
  Self-Catering

Buses

1, 1A, 1B - Tiverton to Exeter via
    Cullompton

Broadclyst, with a population of roughly 1,467 residents, is a charming but small village located 5 miles east of Exeter. Situated in the heart of Killerton's estate, it has both fantastic countryside and woodland areas to enjoy as well as beautiful thatched cottage architecture throughout.

In Broadclyst, you will find The Red Lion Inn located right next to the village green and The New Inn located some distance away just outside the village, to the east. Points of interest include the fifteenth century St. John the Baptist Church and the Clyst Mill. The church hosts an ancient cross and is adorned with gargoyles throughout. The Clyst Mill, like many buildings in this area, is now looked after by the National Trust and still continues to produce award-winning flour.

To continue the walk begin at the front of The Red Lion Inn. Proceed out onto the main road (B3181) and head right. At the first beautifully yellow thatched cottage, take a right turn on to Church Lane. Upon reaching the end, turn left along Sunnyfield. After a few metres turn right down the gravel track as this will lead you down to the turning that takes you on up to Clyston Mill.

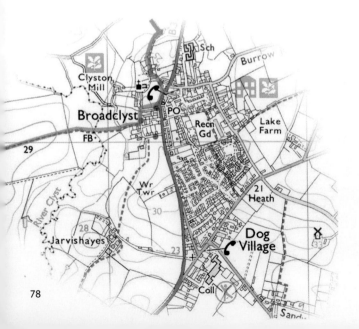

Clyston Mill

Records of a mill named Clyston in Broadclyst can be found as early as 1086 when it was first mentioned in the Domesday book, however, the original mill's location remains a mystery.

The mill that stands today has played an active role for many hundreds of years and still remains busy to this day. During the early parts of the twentieth century, the mill became a very busy place. From 1915 apples were pressed as well as corn and, later, through the 1930s and 1940s water was pumped to a reservoir behind the Red Lion Inn for the village's Monday wash day.

In 1944, the mill was left to the Killerton estate and it continues to make in the region of five to six tons of flour each year. You can taste the award-winning flour by paying a visit to Killerton's restaurant and café.

Grid Ref: SX 980 972

At the end of the track, enter through the gate straight in front of you. Proceed across the fields ensuring you keep to the section with a raised walkway as this will lead you to a small outbuilding. Once at the small building proceed directly straight and cut through the middle of the next field. Upon reaching the wide track, enter into the field straight ahead and follow the narrow track alongside the left hand side of the structure to where you should enter out into a large gravelled clearing.

Leading towards the M5 flyover

At this point, you will be situated right next to the M5 again. Proceed over the bridge and down into Hatchland Road. At the bottom of the crossroads continue straight. You will enter into the east-side of Politmore village. Continue onwards until you arrive at the T-junction directly in front of the St Mary the Virgin Church.

At the junction, turn right and proceed along. Take the second left that leads past Lathy's Farm. Stay on this road as it bends around to the right and leads uphill until you reach the next T-junction. Turn left and follow along the road bypassing the large

coniferous woodland of Huxham Brake. This area is lovely for a peaceful nature filled walk and may be worth a detour if you fancy it.

As you approach the end of Huxham Brake, the road then turns into a steep climb up to the junction where the road joins onto Stoke Hill and where you will spot the 'Welcome to Exeter' sign. Proceed left up and along Stoke Hill taking care to look out for cars. This road is fairly busy as it runs between Stoke Cannon and Exeter's suburb of Pennsylvania.

Looking back up the Exe Valley with the village of Brampford Speke to the left and Stoke Cannon on the right.

At the second large house on your right turn, look out for a footpath sign that points right and follow the track around the side of the grounds of the house. This path starts out as a gravel track where you will be positioned on the ridge above Stoke Woods. You can enjoy more terrific views of the area, this time looking back up the Exe valley from where you previously came from. On a clear day, and if you have good eyesight, you can just about make out the wind turbine that you passed earlier located on top of the hill above Silverton.

As you proceed along this track and grow closer to Stoke Hill Farm, the path turns into a sodden mud bath where the ground has been churned up. This section also acts as a bridleway for horse riders so take care and stick to the edges as best you can.

When you reach the front of Stoke Hill Farm, turn left and enter into the drive. Head along the side of the building. At the end of the building, turn right back onto the muddy footpath that leads up to the base of Stoke Hill Fort; this is one of Exeter's highest point.

Head down passing Rollestone Farm until you eventually enter out on to Pennsylvania Road. From here, you will leave the muddy trails behind as the remainder of the trail is predominately tarmac, with the exception of a few short sections.

Turn right then at the junction turn left along Pennsylvania Road. Head straight keeping right at the first turning at Rosebarn Lane. At this point, it is all downhill. As you venture onwards down Pennsylvania Road, you will spot the occasional sign secured to

Exeter flood relief channel

lampposts confirming that you are on the Two Counties Way. Down this road, you will pass some beautiful Georgian houses as well as Pennsylvania park. You will also pass the grounds of Exeter University on your right.

Exeter Floods

In the 1960s flooding devastated the areas of Exwick and St Thomas. The water level reached its deepest at places such as Oakhampton Street where water reached a height of six foot. After recovering from the floods, plans were drawn up for a flood prevention scheme. In total three flood relief channels were eventually built. The Exwick spillway is the largest and most technically complex of the three as it has a huge gate that is designed to close water from the river and divert it into the spillway, a fully automated process.

When you finally arrive the crossroads and traffic lights, turn right along onto the Prince of Wales Road and proceed along. Take the left directly after the cricket ground. From here, the path runs next to a cycle lane and along a ridge that cuts along the south side above the Taddiforde Brook. This brook runs through the boundary of the university campus to join with the River Exe. At the end of the joint pedestrian and cycle path, climb the gate straight ahead that leads into the meadow and head down and cross over the Brook. Again this section can become quite muddy with wet weather. Once over, head left and follow the path as it leads up to and enters out onto Streatham Drive. Turn left and proceed to the end of the road.

From the traffic lights, head up and pass by The Imperial pub and cross over at the zebra crossing. Take the next right onto Howell Road and, at the bottom of the hill, turn left onto St David's Hill. Keep straight. Once you have passed The Great Western Hotel, cross over to the left-hand side and head around to the left. Cross over the busy railway tracks that lead into St David's Station. Next, proceed along Station Road and cross the bridge over the River Exe. Once over the Exeter flood relief channel, take the left that leads down to bring you to the edge of the channel.

From here, simply follow alongside the canal downstream for the 2.3 kilometres to Exeter's Quayside. This section of path along the channel is very popular for leisure activities with cyclists, runners, dog walkers, and rowers who frequently pass up and down the canal. Once the channel joins back up with the Exe, continue passing underneath Exe bridges and round the final bend to be brought into the southern side of Exeter's historic quay.

LEG 10 - EXETER (QUAY) TO STARCROSS

Exeter Quayside

Exeter (Quay)

OS Grid Ref: SX 9202 9201
District: Exeter
OS Explorer map:
114 - Exeter & the Exe Valley

Leg Distance: 17.1 km / 10.6 miles
Elevation Gain: 87m

Points of interest
- Custom House Visitor Centre
- The Boat Shed Theatre
- Saddles & Paddles Bike Hire

Accommodation & Eateries
- On The Waterfront
- Samuel Jones Smoke & Ale House
- The Ridge Coffee Shop
- Bar Venezia
- Jolly Rogers Cafe
- The Prospect Inn
- The Coffee Cellar
- Boatyard Café and Bakery
- The Welcome Café
- Globe Backpackers
- White Hart
- Hotel du Vin

Buses
Main Bus Station (Located in the city centre)

Exeter is the county capital and has much to explore. From the 1,000-year-old cathedral to the hidden tunnels that lay beneath the streets, it is a fun city to explore. The city centre itself is roughly only a 20-minute walk, however, Exeter's Quayside has an abundance of amenities to enjoy on both sides of the river in the form of numerous cafes, bars, and restaurants.

The Quay has a long history associated with the city dating back thousands of years. Even when the Romans arrived the Exe would have been navigable. In 1248, the Courtenay family built a weir across the river and forced ships to dock at Topsham, this is what led to the creation of the canal. In 1563, plans were set in motion for a canal to be built linking Countess Weir to the city. In the hundred years that followed, the trade brought great wealth to the city on the back of the wool trade. The arrival of the railways caused all shipping to decline. Today, the only boats that frequent the quay are canoes and pedaloes, and the small yachts laid up in the basin. Much of the quay area has been regenerated over recent years and is now a vibrant location for outdoor activities and tourists.

On this final leg of this journey, to press on from Exeter's Quayside, ensure you cross over to the right side of the river by passing over the bridge. Alternatively, if you want a more novel way of crossing, you could even use the hand operated cable ferry known as Butts Ferry. This can found just down from the suspension bridge. It has been in operation since 1641, though today can only be used in the summer.

Continue along the edge of the river by passing Haven Banks Outdoor Centre and the boatyard on your right until you arrive at the floodgate.

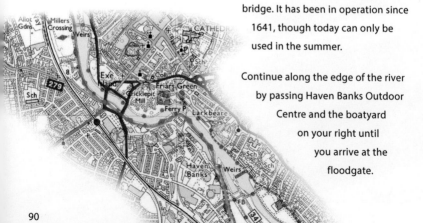

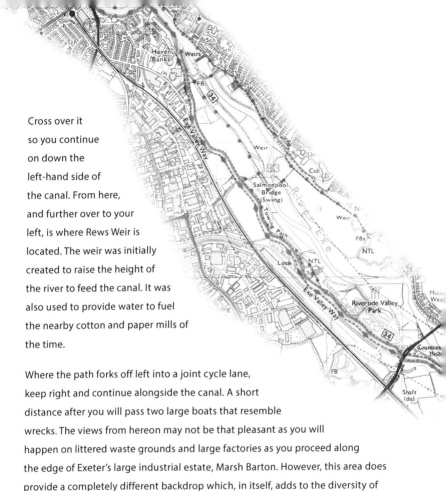

Cross over it
so you continue
on down the
left-hand side of
the canal. From here,
and further over to your
left, is where Rews Weir is
located. The weir was initially
created to raise the height of
the river to feed the canal. It was
also used to provide water to fuel
the nearby cotton and paper mills of
the time.

Where the path forks off left into a joint cycle lane,
keep right and continue alongside the canal. A short
distance after you will pass two large boats that resemble
wrecks. The views from hereon may not be that pleasant as you will
happen on littered waste grounds and large factories as you proceed along
the edge of Exeter's large industrial estate, Marsh Barton. However, this area does
provide a completely different backdrop which, in itself, adds to the diversity of
the experience of the entire walk.

When you finally reach the next lock continue straight ahead, again keeping to
the left-hand side of the canal. This is where you also join a road that leads all the
way down to the double locks. It is here that the surrounding area becomes a little
more pleasant as you proceed into the nature reserve, Riverside Country Park,
which offers green open spaces for an abundance of wildlife. Here you can find

M5 bridge over the River Exe

popular cycle routes and several attractive circular walks to choose from. Head along the road until you reach the first of two canal pubs, The Double Locks.

On leaving The Double Locks, it does not matter a great deal which way to proceed so you can pass down either the left or right-hand side of the canal to where you will eventually arrive at Bridge Road and to that of Countess Weir Swing Bridges.

Important! Upon reaching the bridges cross over to the opposite side and ensure that you continue onwards down the right-hand side of the canal. If you remain on the left, the path comes to an abrupt end a little distance after the entrance to the sewage works. As you continue along, the canal arcs to the right then curves back round to the left before heading onwards to pass under the M5 motorway bridge.

Countess Weir Swing Bridges

The bridges played a crucial role in the planning and preparations for the D-Day attacks in May 1944. They were used for a total of 3 days and nights for the rehearsals of the glider-borne attacks on the famous Pegasus Bridge, over the river Canal de Caen, carried out by the Buckinghamshire Light Infantry which took place the night of 5/6 June 1944.

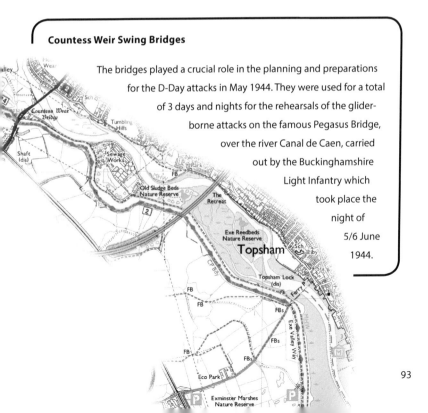

Topsham Ferry Crossing

This stretch of canal is particularly popular with fishermen so take care not to get in their way.

From passing under the M5 you will notice over to the other side of the Estuary the village of Topsham. Further down you will arrive at the Topsham Lock; from here the Topsham ferry runs across the River Exe between the lock and Ferry Road in Topsham. Times of operation does depend on weather conditions but runs daily except on Tuesdays during the Summer and weekends in the winter. Just next to the lock is also the small but quirky Topsham Lock Cottage which doubles up as a café and holiday let.

From the lock, the route heads right into the field. As the following section heads through part of the Exminster Marshes Nature Reserve, the route can become very muddy and wet as it is essentially a wild wetland. If you feel like a more relaxed walk then you could continue onwards down the side of the canal to arrive at the Turf Locks, the second and final canal pub.

Otherwise, the Marshes are a valuable and important reserve for wading birds, wintering ducks and geese. It, therefore, offers a fantastic opportunity to soak up the sights and sounds of the vast array of birds and wildlife. This is the way this book will follow.

Enter right into the reserve and head in the direction of the small footbridges. As you pass over them and through several fields you will soon enter out onto Station Road. Here, proceed right and continue straight. Eventually, take the left that leads into the car park of Exminster Marshes, bordering to the railway line. Head to the bottom of the car park and enter through into the walkway. The path then runs parallel with the railway line for approximately one kilometre before bending to the left. Follow it round then cross over and enter into the adjacent field. From here, you will be able to see the Turf Locks in the distance. Head along the faint worn path that cuts directly across this field to the gate and enter out to the west facing side of the Turf Locks to be greeted with the final set of locks and to where the Exeter Canal flows out and merges into the Exe Estuary.

Leading away from The Turf Locks, follow the path round slightly to the right then take a left onto the path that leads along the top of the bank. This allows for a much more scenic walk along the estuary and provides wonderful views across over to Exmouth. Upon reaching the joint pedestrian and cycle bridge, cross back over the railway line for the final time and proceed along the path until you arrive at Church road. Soon enough, you will arrive in front of St Clement's Church.

Turn right and head along to the end of Church Road and at the bend. Head straight up the grass bank and through the gate into the fenced walkway. From here, the path leads up and over the perimeter of Powderham Park.

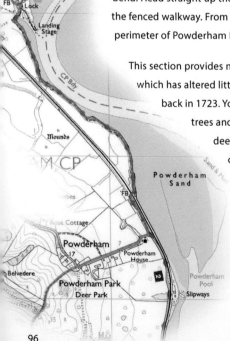

This section provides more fantastic views of the Deer Park which has altered little since it was first depicted on a map back in 1723. You are sure to find a diverse range of trees and will be able to see the herd of fallow deer (about 600 of them) that have been continuously kept since 1723. Upon reaching the road that runs through to the Powderham Estate Office, cross directly over and continue along the footpath, firstly crossing over the River Kenn, and onwards through the residential area until you enter out on to Fore Street (A379) that runs directly through the village of Kenton.

Powderham Castle

Powderham Castle stems from the ancient Dutch word polder, aptly meaning "the hamlet of the reclaimed marshland". It is believed the manor house that first occupied this site was first built by Sir Philip Courtenay sometime after 1390 but has exchanged hands and appearances several times since. It was turned into a castle around the seventeenth century though never gained a moat or keep. Famously, during the Civil War, three-hundred Royalist soldiers garrisoned the Castle. An initial attempt to attach by the Parliamentarians failed, but it finally fell in 1646 and remained badly damaged until the eighteenth century.

Today, the castle is still owned by the Courtenay family. It is used to host weddings and concerts – it even hosted BBC Radio One's Big Weekend in May 2016 with Coldplay headlining! Overall, it is worth a gander to ponder the history that unfolded on this site and the fantastic sounds it has heard.

The Turf Locks

The village of Kenton

Cross over to the opposite side of the road and proceed past The Dolphin Inn, heading towards the large church. Keep left and enter Church Street then take the first left onto Mamhead Road. After a few metres, and on the bend, again turn left on to Pit Hill where there is a sharp incline leading up to Witcombe Lane. At the junction, turn left onto Witcombe Lane and follow the road along as it runs below the A379 as it leads onwards away from Kenton.

Keep left at the next fork in the road and follow the road round for the final few hundred metres entering through the western side of Starcross's residential area. As you join up with Staplake Road, turn right to join back up with the A379; the Strand carpark will be located directly in front of you. At this junction, again, turn right to finally arrive at the finishing point of this beautiful and diverse trail, the village of Starcross.

To reach the rail station and bus stop continue along a few extra metres from the Strand Car Park to where you can find them located near to Brunel's Atmospheric Pumping station.

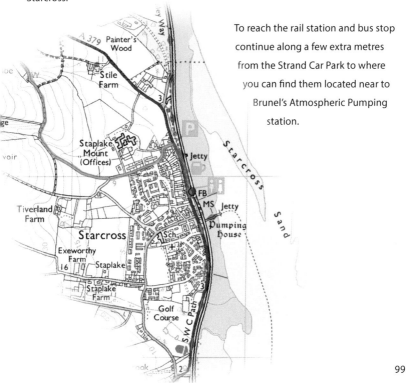

FINISHING AT STARCROSS

Starcross Train Station

Starcross

OS Grid Ref: SX 9770 8187
District: Teignbridge
OS Explorer map:
OL44 - Torquay & Dawlish

Points of interest

- Starcross to Exmouth ferry
- Brunel Pumping House
- Cockwood Harbour

Accommodation & Eateries

- The Atmospheric Railway Inn
- The Galleon Inn
- Convenience Store
- Fish & Chip Shop
- The Royal British Legion
- Hunters Lodge Caravan and Camping Site
- River Exe Cafe
- The Croft Guest House - (nearby Cockwood)
- The Anchor Inn - (nearby Cockwood)

Buses

2 - Exeter to Newton Abbot

Starcross, situated on the western shore of the Exe Estuary, is home to approximately 1,780 residents. The village, and its surrounding areas become extremely popular in the summer months with holidaymakers descending on the area for its beauty and leisure time activities.

In Starcross, you will find a convenience store as well as The Atmospheric Railway Inn, The Galleon Inn and a fish & chip takeaway located all within a short distance of the railway station. If you feel up to exploring a bit more of the area, I would highly recommend taking a walk to the small harbor located in Cockwood. Here you will find The Anchor and Ship Inn - a great place to sit out on the harbor wall and sample a well-deserved refreshing pint.

You can refer to page 21 to find out further information on transport options when leaving Starcross. Otherwise, if you had more time and felt up to exploring further sections of the Exe Estuary, you could even catch the Starcross ferry across the other side to Exmouth if you so wished. Note though that the ferry does only run certain times of the year so it would be worth checking timetables beforehand. Trains and buses frequently run between Exmouth and Exeter and the rail journey itself also provides a beautiful coastal jaunt.

Starcross Pumping Station

A notable feature of Starcross is the impressive surviving building from one of the great Victorian engineers, Isambard Kingdom Brunel. The pumping station was one of eleven to be built; it helped to propel trains along the section of track between Exeter and Plymouth by a system of atmospheric traction.

The atmospheric system of traction involved the train being propelled along by a piston in a tube laid between rails. The traction system was plagued by technical difficulties from the start and became a lot more expensive to run than the conventional system of the time, it subsequently closed for good less than a year later. It is now home to one of the country's oldest sailing clubs, the Starcross Fishing and Cruising Club.

Starcross Pumping Station

USEFUL INFORMATION

ORGANISATIONS

Visit Somerset
Web: www.visitsomerset.co.uk
Facebook: @visitsomersetuk
Twitter: @VisitSomerset

Visit Devon
Web: www.visitdevon.co.uk
Facebook: @VisitDevon
Twitter: @VisitDevon

Taunton Deane Council
Web: www.tauntondeane.gov.uk
Facebook: @tauntondeanebc
Twitter: @TDBC

Mid Devon
Web: www.middevon.gov.uk
Facebook: @middevon1
Twitter: @MidDevonDC
Email: customerfirst@middevon.gov.uk

Exeter City Council
Web: www.exeter.gov.uk
Facebook: @ExeterCityCouncil
Twitter: @ExeterCouncil
Email: customer.services@exeter.gov.uk

Teignbridge Council
Web: www.teignbridge.gov.uk
Facebook: @Teignbridge
Twitter: @Teignbridge
Email: info@teignbridge.gov.uk

English Heritage
Web: www.english-heritage.org.uk
Facebook: @englishheritage
Twitter: @EnglishHeritage
Phone: 0370 333 1181
Email: customers@english-heritage.org.uk

National Trust
Web: www.nationaltrust.org.uk
Facebook: @nationaltrust
Twitter: @nationaltrust
Phone: 0344 800 1895
Email: enquiries@nationaltrust.org.uk

Ramblers
Web: www.ramblers.org.uk
Facebook: @ramblers
Twitter: @RamblersGB
Phone: 020 7339 8500
Email: ramblers@ramblers.org.uk

COMMUNITY INFORMATION

Taunton
Web: www.visitsomerset.co.uk/taunton

Bradford on Tone
Web: www.bradfordontone.co.uk

Wellington
Web: www.wellingtonsomerset.com

Sampford Peverell
Web: www.sampfordpeverell.org.uk

Tiverton
Web: www.exploretiverton.co.uk

Bickleigh
Web: www.bickleigh.org.uk

Silverton
Web: www.silvertonparishcouncil.co.uk

Broadclyst
Web: www.broadclyst.org

Exeter
Web: www.visitexeter.com

Starcross
Web: www.starcrosspc.org.uk

PUBLIC TRANSPORTATION

National Rail Enquiries
Web: www.nationalrail.co.uk
Phone: 03457 48 49 50

National Express
Web: www.nationalexpress.com/en
Phone: 0871 781 8181

First Bus
Web: www.firstgroup.com/somerset
Phone: 0345 602 0121

Somerset bus routes
Web: www.firstgroup.com/uploads/maps/
network_map.pdf

Traveline
Web: www.traveline.info
Phone: 0871 200 2233

Stagecoach
Web: www.stagecoachbus.com
Email: southwest.enquiries@
stagecoachbus.com
Phone: 01392 42 77 11

Interactive Devon bus routes
Web: www.traveldevon.info/bus/
interactive-bus-map/

TAXIS

Taunton and the Taunton Dean area

Leo Taxis
Phone: 01823 924400

Cotford Cabs
Phone: 07517 480141

Archie's Cabs
Phone: 01823 428844

Starcross and the Teignbridge Area

Black Swan Taxis
Phone: 01626 786786

Grab A Cab
Phone: 01626 866668

Kemp's Cabs
Phone: 01626 888111

Tiverton and the Mid Devon Area

Parkway Taxis
Phone: 01884 38899

Loids Taxis
Phone: 07966 247253

A2B Taxis
Phone: 07971 275322

ADDITIONAL INFO

Tiverton Canal Co
Web: www.tivertoncanal.co.uk
Phone: 01884 253345

Grand Western Canal Pub Guide
Web: www.canalandriversidepubs.
co.uk/Grand-Western.htm

Exmouth to Starcross Ferry
Web: www.facebook.com/
StarcrossExmouthFerry
Phone: 01626 774770

Devon Walking Trails
Web: www.devon.gov.uk/ddwalking.pdf

Somerset Walking Trails
Web: www.somerset.gov.
uk/environment-and-
planning/rights-of-way/
walks-and-trails-in-somerset/

EMERGENCY SERVICES

Exmoor Search and Rescue
If an emergency, dial 999 and ask for police.
Web: www.exmoor-srt.org.uk
Facebook: @exmoorsearchandrescueteam
Twitter: @ExmoorSRT
Email: info@exmoor-srt.org.uk

Exmouth RNLI
If an emergency, dial 999.
Web: www.exmouthlifeboat.org.uk
Facebook: @exmouthrnli
Twitter: @ExmouthRNLI
Email: rnliexmouthshop@gmail.com

NOTES:

NOTES:

Printed in Great Britain
by Amazon